Maxwell Eaton III

BEAR BUILDS A HOUSE

NEAL PORTER BOOKS
HOLIDAY HOUSE / NEW YORK

SIE·KEE·EEE

With special thanks
to Cameron Clark—skilled carpenter, tolerant neighbor

Neal Porter Books

Text and illustrations copyright © 2022 by Maxwell Eaton III

All Rights Reserved

HOLIDAY HOUSE is registered in the U.S. Patent and Trademark Office.

Printed and bound in October 2021 at Toppan Leefung, DongGuan, China.

The artwork for this book was created with watercolor and graphite pencil

on 140 lb. bright white cold press watercolor paper.

Book design by Jennifer Browne

www.holidayhouse.com

First Edition

1 3 5 7 9 10 8 6 4 2

Library of Congress Cataloging-in-Publication Data

Names: Eaton, Maxwell, III, author, illustrator.

Title: Bear builds a house / by Maxwell Eaton III.

Description: First edition. | New York : Holiday House, [2022] | "A Neal

Porter book." | Audience: Ages 4 to 8. | Audience: Grades K–1. |

Summary: "Bear sets out to build a house from scratch before winter

comes"— Provided by publisher.

Identifiers: LCCN 2021004194 | ISBN 9780823447145 (hardcover)

Subjects: LCSH: House construction—Juvenile literature.

Classification: LCC TH4811.5 .E27 2022 | DDC 690/.837—dc23

LC record available at https://lccn.loc.gov/2021004194

ISBN: 978-0-8234-4714-5 (hardcover)

Spring has arrived, and Bear is on the move . . .

She's been caring for a friend's house, but now it's time to build one of her own. It will take thoughtful planning, mountains of hard work, and a few good friends to get it done before the snow falls again. And it all starts now!

Bear has already found her site and set up a temporary shelter. Though no location is perfect, this one will suit Bear's needs nicely.

Bear draws up a site plan using the measurements she's taken. When deciding where the house should go, she needs to consider everything she'd like to build this year as well as everything she may ever want to build in the future. It's better to plan now since she can't just move her house later on.

Next, Bear needs to plan the actual house. She could go to an architect, but Bear is one handy mammal. The trick will be designing a house large enough for her to eat, sleep, work, and relax in without making it so large that it's difficult to heat or too costly and time-consuming to build.

Bear also draws up elevations. These are what the house will look like from each side once it's completed.

The planning is finished! It's time for Bear to get to work. But not by herself. She'll have some friends helping, each with a special set of skills that will move the project along quickly, safely, and successfully.

They are happy to help because Bear has helped her friends many times in the past and will continue to do so in the future. That's the Better Bear Bargain!

Bear's job will be to focus on planning, staying organized, communicating, coordinating, scheduling, and working alongside her friends.

The next step is TIMBER! Beaver and Bear begin cutting down beautiful straight white pines, perfect to mill into lumber. The spaces they leave behind will allow more sunlight to come into the house.

Beaver brings in his portable sawmill, and the whole gang works together moving the logs onto the deck of the mill where each board is cut according to Bear's list.

2" x 6" x 8' means the board is 2 inches thick, 6 inches wide, and 8 feet long.

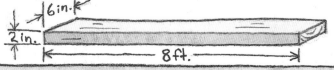

Using chainsaws, they cut (or "fell") each tree, then saw off (or "limb") the branches and cut (or "buck") the logs to length. Eight-, twelve-, and sixteen-foot logs are common lengths for building houses.

Look at that beautiful stack of lumber! The wood is heavy with sap and moisture like a wet towel and will need to dry out (or "season") for at least a few months. Luckily, Bear has plenty of other things to do.

Now for the foundation. It's the most important part of the house, because it supports absolutely everything. Bear has a few options.

Full foundation

Crawl space foundation

Pier foundation

Bear decides to build the house on concrete piers. She and Woodchuck can dig the holes themselves and pour the concrete without large, expensive machinery.

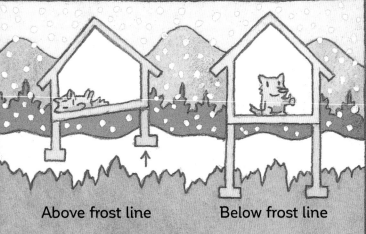

Above frost line

Below frost line

They will make the piers deeper than where the ground freezes each winter. A foundation below the frost line is less likely to shift as the soil freezes and thaws.

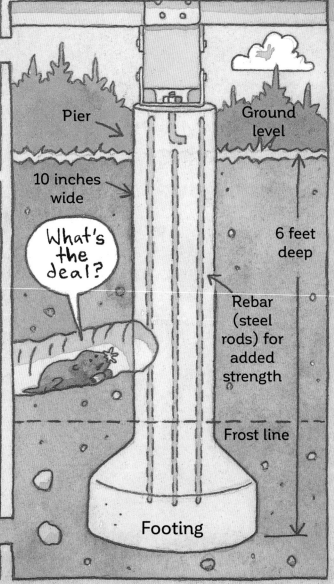

Pier

Ground level

10 inches wide

What's the deal?

6 feet deep

Rebar (steel rods) for added strength

Frost line

Footing

Bear and Woodchuck set to work laying out exactly where each pier will go, digging holes six feet deep, mixing concrete with water in a wheelbarrow, and then pouring it into cardboard tubes called "forms" before letting it harden.

Bear and Woodchuck head up the hill to the spring where clean water flows right out of the ground. They kept an eye on it all last year and it never dried up or froze. It's also in a good location uphill from the homesite (no pumps needed) and away from other houses, salted roads, and animal pastures that could contaminate the water. Here is what Bear and Woodchuck accomplish with stones, mortar, pipes, some soggy feet, and a whole lot of digging.

Where will the water go?

Fresh water is flowing, but where will it go once it heads down the sink or shower drain? In this case, back where it came from—the ground. Bear and Woodchuck dig three trenches and bury a hole-filled pipe in gravel to create a "leach field." Used water from the house will travel through the pipe, out the holes, and into the soil.

* All underground

Fresh water to house

Drainpipe from house

The leach field*

Distribution box

Holes in drainpipe

Gravel

Small tank

Where water will enter house

Foundation pier

The outhouse

Toilet seat

Waste

An insulated box will protect water from the cold as it rises.

I like to keep it even simpler than that.

But where does everything *else* go? Outside to the outhouse! Bear prefers the simplicity and environmental benefits of going to the bathroom over a hole in the ground covered by a shed.

Bear is going to build a stick-frame house. This consists of closely spaced boards that support the house like a skeleton. The lumber has seasoned. Let's start framing!

The floor is built first. Using just a handsaw, a framing hammer, a combination square, and some nails, Bear assembles boards spaced sixteen inches apart over the foundation.

Handsaw

Nails

Framing hammer

Combination square

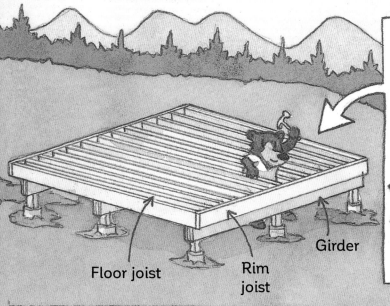

Floor joist

Rim joist

Girder

Next, Bear lays down the subfloor. She's using one-inch-thick boards nailed down across the joists. Now she'll have something to walk on.

Subfloor

Up with the walls! Bear builds each wall flat on the subfloor, leaving openings for windows and doors. Then she stands it up and nails it in place, making sure it's perfectly vertical with the aid of a level.

Level

Air bubble indicates vertical surface

And nuts for squirrels, please.

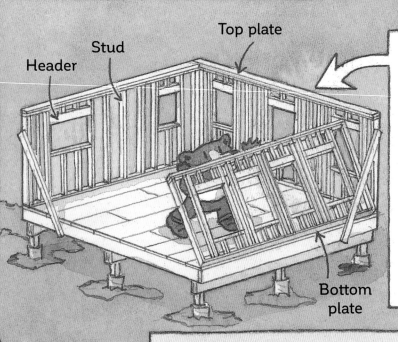

Header

Stud

Top plate

Bottom plate

Remember: joists for floors, studs for walls, rafters for roofs.

With the exterior complete, Bear and her friends can start work inside without worrying about the weather. And speaking of weather, they've finished just in time.

While Bear is finishing up outside, Bobcat is working hard inside on all things pipe-related. From the water line she runs cold water plumbing (blue) to the water heater, kitchen sink, bathroom sink, and shower; hot water plumbing (red) from the water heater to the sinks and shower; propane fuel line (yellow) to the water heater, cook stove, and refrigerator; and, finally, a drainpipe (white) from the kitchen and bathroom drains down and out to the leach field. Whew!

Plastic pipe

Crimp ring

Barb coupling

Crimp tool

Many homes have water pipes made of copper. For Bear's house, Bobcat is using flexible plastic pipes joined by tight metal rings.

Propane-powered fridge

Cook stove

I just remembered cats don't like water.

Sink

Liquid propane fuel tank

Water heater

Pipe from spring

Trap

Drainpipe

The sun is back, and the timing couldn't be better. Raccoon has wired the house to a photovoltaic system. The electric lights and outlets will get their power from another world—the sun! Here's how it works:

Lay it on me.

SUN
Rains down light particles called photons.

Photons (they're small and fast)

Does the sun really have a face?

Do raccoons really wear pants?

SOLAR PANEL
Showering photons collide with electrons inside the panel. The electrons are then channeled together to generate electrical current.

Now try!

ELECTRICAL WIRE
Conducts electrical current.

Electricity

They call me Sparky.

Who does?

Nobody.

Bear is so close! Still inside, she pushes layers (or "batts") of fiberglass insulation into the spaces between each stud, joist, and rafter. This will help keep heat trapped inside like a puffy goose-down coat.

You've got a lot of nerve.

Bits of fiberglass can irritate skin, lungs, and eyes. Bear plays it safe with gloves, a mask, and eye protection.

The walls are functionally finished, but who wants to look at fiberglass? Bear decides to cover the walls, ceiling, and floor with tongue-and-groove boards (milled by Beaver). She nails them one at a time across the studs and rafters from floor to ceiling before doing the same across the subfloor.

Tongue

Groove

Tongue-and-groove boards

Ack! Is that snow?!

It's sawdust.

Yes. You keep saying that.

Bear then seals the deal with trim boards to clean up the rough cuts, uneven ends, and occasional gaps. She is *almost* done!

The kitchen and bathroom cabinets and appliances are installed. There's just one last job to do, and it's going to require the entire crew.

It has been a long spring, summer, and fall, but it's finally time for . . .

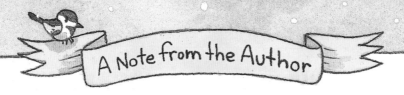

A Note from the Author

Bear crafted a practical home using a mix of old and new tools, technologies, and materials best suited to her environment, resources, time, abilities, pace, taste, and style. A beautiful reflection of herself.

But while she did her best to work with renewable materials and energy close to home, Bear's structure is not as "off grid" as it may appear. Fiberglass insulation, copper wiring, batteries, metal roofing, new glass windows, plastic plumbing, and concrete are all incredibly resource intensive. A house like this may leave Bear's neck of the woods with nothing more than a few stumps, but somewhere in the world there are serious trade-offs, many of which will ultimately affect Bear right where she lives.

It is Bear's responsibility to continue to minimize the continually harmful inputs within her own system (in this case, propane fuel and a parade of short-lived electronics), while striving toward an existence in which her only impact is a positive one for her community and the planet on which she lives.

Further reading

Housebuilding for Children: Step-by-Step Plans for Houses Children Can Build Themselves, Lester Walker, The Overlook Press, 1977.

Mill, David Macaulay, Houghton Mifflin Harcourt, 1989.

Tools for Conviviality, Ivan Illich, Harper & Row, 1973.